Book Description

Are you obsessed with the horrific crimes of some of the worst serial killers of our time? Do you want to know what makes these murderers tick and why they committed their notorious crimes?

Serial murder is one of the most terrifying and fascinating types of crime we can imagine, and there is no doubt that many of us are deeply interested in the people behind these seasons of terror.

Sadly, as we evolve as a society, we seem to be producing more and more of these predators. Why is this, and how do we determine which are the most notorious?

In *The 10 Most Notorious Serial Killers of All Time*, you will learn about a group of men whose crimes will go down in history as some of the worst ever uncovered.

In *The 10 Most Notorious Serial Killers of All Time*, you will discover:

- Which 10 serial killers make the list.
- Why some of these murderers, despite not having the highest victim count, will forever haunt our nightmares.

- Which serial killers stepped beyond the realm of the terrible into unthinkable acts of necrophilia and cannibalism.
- If anything in these killers' pasts point to a root cause for their crimes.

If you are obsessed with true crime and serial killer research, this book has all the information you've ever wanted on the worst of the worst.

To learn which 10 serial killers are the most notorious of all time, click "add to cart" now!

The 10 Most Notorious Serial Killers of All Time

An Insight into the Minds of History's Worst Serial Killers, and What Drove Them to Commit such Terrible Crimes

Paragon Publishing

from various sources. Please consult a licensed professional before attempting any techniques outlined in this book.

By reading this document, the reader agrees that under no circumstances is the author responsible for any losses, direct or indirect, that are incurred as a result of the use of the information contained within this document, including, but not limited to, errors, omissions, or inaccuracies.

Table of Contents

Introduction

"We serial killers are your sons, we are your husbands, we are everywhere. And there will be more of your children dead tomorrow." —Ted Bundy

In the world of true crime, there is perhaps no type of criminal that is more intriguing and horrifying, in equal parts, than the serial killer. Although murder—the taking of a human life—is the most difficult crime to comprehend, we can sometimes come to terms with individual murders. At times, crimes of passion or one-off murders in the course of a robbery, for instance, although still shocking and terribly tragic, are almost comprehensible. Every human being has a line and sometimes circumstances can push people over that line with tragic consequences. Those crimes we can study, understand, and put into a neat little box.

Then, there are serial killers.

These are men, and occasionally women, who kill, often viciously, again and again, stopping only when they are caught by law enforcement. Serial killers and their crimes are the most intriguing phenomena in the true crime world and those interested in the genre devour every piece of information that can be found about these criminals.

Even within the serial killer corner, though, there are some that are seemingly worse than their peers. The worst of the worst are not always those with the highest victim count. Sometimes it is simply the cold-blooded viciousness of the killer's acts that puts them in the top ten.

The ten men we will discuss in this book have all killed without conscience. As you will discover, they all come from very different backgrounds and used diverse methods of killing. In the chapters that follow, you will be introduced to ten men in increasing increments of notoriety. We will learn why these murderers are considered some of the worst serial killers of all time, how they hunted and struck down their victims, and what led them to these depths of depravity.

#10: Pedro Alonso Lopez

The young girl walks along the dirt road in the scorching Colombian sun. Her feet drag in the sand and she plays a game with herself to pass the time. Her mother has sent her to the neighboring village to trade some fruit for flour. She didn't mind the walk, the sun was hot, though, and the dense jungle to the side of the path looked inviting with its cool shade. Then the trees rustled and a man appeared. He had a kind face and beckoned to the girl to join him in the shade for a while. Her dragging footsteps in the dirt ended there and she disappeared without a trace. The Monster of the Andes has struck again.

The Early Days

Pedro Alonso Lopez was born in Santa Isabel, Columbia on October 8th, 1948. Pedro's mother, Benilda, was just three months pregnant with him when his father, Medardo Reyes was killed in an armed conflict in Colombia. Pedro was the seventh child of 13 children, and his father's death had an immediate and ongoing impact on the entire family, before Pedro had even taken his first breath.

After Medardo's death, it's alleged that Benilda turned to the sex trade to support her children and she would fall pregnant and bear the children of several of her clients after Pedro's birth. There are two very distinct narratives behind Pedro's childhood and, as it often does, the truth probably lies somewhere between the two tales.

In one retelling, Pedro was the victim of a physically abusive mother and after years of violent, poverty-ridden misery, he ran away from home. In the other version, Pedro was a bad apple from the start and he was asked to leave the home after he was found to be sexually abusing his younger sister.

In later years, though, Pedro's mother would support neither of these narratives, simply saying that her son was a polite boy and that he wanted to be a teacher when he grew up. It is often difficult to get accurate information about the childhood experiences of serial killers as anyone with a stake in the matter would want their version to be what goes down in the history books. Parents, for the most part, find it difficult to admit that anything they may have done contributed to their offspring's horrific crimes. The killer, of course, especially during the trial phase, needs to appear a victim, so it would be beneficial to them if judges, juries, and the public at large believed that their crimes were the product of years of abuse.

This is not to say that many serial killers have not experienced significant neglect or abuse as children, but it is important for us to keep in mind that a frighteningly large number of people will suffer some form of abuse during their childhood, but very few will go on to become serial killers.

Whether Pedro left his family home by force or by choice, we do know that he was soon living on the streets. In Bogota, the capital of Colombia, he joined the large groups of homeless children known as "gamines." Pedro eventually joined a gang and started to smoke basuco, a form of street cocaine. He would later say that he had been the victim of sexual assault by a man who had pretended to offer him a safe place to sleep, and instead took Pedro to an abandoned building and raped him.

When Pedro was 10-years-old, he says that an American couple found him on the streets and took him into their home. They enrolled him in a school for orphans, but while he was there, he was molested by a teacher. He ran away at the age of 12.

As Lopez moved into his teens, he was no longer looked at by members of the public as an endearing child and he says he found it more and more difficult to find anyone willing to help him. As is the case with many serial killers, Pedro started out with petty crimes, but soon graduated to car theft. By the time he was 18 years old, he was arrested and imprisoned for the first time. Pedro claims that, while in prison, he was raped by two fellow inmates and he turned on his attackers, killing them. Reports differ as to whether Pedro was given additional jail time for these murders, but these are believed to be his first two victims (Biography.com editors, 2014).

The Murders Begin

When Pedro was released from prison, it is alleged that he started to hunt young girls. He would usually choose girls from poor backgrounds, perhaps because their families would not have the resources needed to look for the girls when they disappeared.

It is difficult to believe that Pedro had not committed any crimes of a sexual nature before he went to prison, as the escalation from car theft to the serial rape and murder of minors does not "fit" with what we know about the evolution of serial killers. It is far more likely that the initial reports of Pedro having molested his younger sister are true and there may well have been other sexual crimes of this nature before he was imprisoned for car theft. Often what we see with serial killers, whose crimes have a sexual motivation, is that they may start out committing rapes or sexual assaults, get caught for those crimes, and be sent to jail for a short period, and then, on being released, they decide they will never go back to prison again. As a result, they decide, not to stop raping, but instead ensure that their victims are unable to report them, and so, they escalate to murder.

In Pedro's case, he did something else that is different from what we typically see in serial killers—he moved geographic areas. Serial killers will usually operate in a geographic area that is well-known to them. This may be an area near where they live, work, or an area with personal significance.

We do not know if Peru held any particular significance to Pedro, or if he had travelled to the country prior to being released from prison. Pedro's modus operandi was to lure his young victims to remote areas, where he would rape and murder them. He seems to have run rampant during the 1970s and would later claim that he had taken dozens of victims in Peru during this time. He soon targeted a nine-year-old girl from the Ayachucos community and when he was caught attempting to lure the girl away, the community turned on him. According to their tribal law, for his crime, Pedro was to be buried alive, but a Western missionary convinced the community to instead hand Pedro over to the police. The Peruvian police had no proof that Pedro had committed any crime other than the attempted kidnapping of the nine-year-old in their country, so they simply deported him back to Columbia.

Back in Columbia, Pedro continued to kill and then moved countries once again. This time, he chose Ecuador as his hunting ground. Families in Ecuador tried to find their missing girls on their own. One mother even placed ads in the local newspaper in an attempt to locate her child.

In 1980, Pedro would eventually make the mistake of targeting the wrong child at a busy market in the Ambato region of Ecuador. A vendor at the market, Carlina Ramon, and a group of her friends, caught him trying to lure Carlina's daughter away from the market. They called police and Pedro was taken into custody (Biography.com editors, 2014).

The Investigation and Conviction

When in police custody, Pedro refused to cooperate. Eventually, Ecuadorian police put one of their investigators undercover as a fellow inmate in the same prison as Pedro. The investigator was able to gain Pedro's trust and the man began to confess and reveal where some of his victims were buried. The enormity of Pedro Lopez's crimes only then became clear.

Police were eventually able to unearth 57 bodies throughout Ecuador, Peru, and Colombia. These discoveries, combined with Pedro's confessions, resulted in Pedro being ultimately charged with 110 murders. Pedro, however, claimed to be responsible for more than 200 deaths in all three countries.

On July 31st, 1981, 33-year-old Pedro Lopez plead guilty to the murder of the 57 girls whose bodies had been recovered. Shockingly, due to Ecuadorian laws at the time, he could only be given the maximum sentence of 16 years in prison. Ecuadorian authorities would later increase this to 25 years. Pedro was imprisoned in Ambato, Ecuador and he was officially diagnosed as a sociopath.

On August 31st, 1994, Pedro Lopez, who was by then dubbed "The Monster of the Andes", in reference to the mountain range which spanned the three countries he had killed in, was released from jail. He had served just 14 years of his sentence and had received an early release for good behavior.

Ecuadorian authorities immediately deported the man to Colombia and authorities there attempted to convict on a murder they believed he had committed 20 years before. Instead, Pedro was found to be legally insane and in 1995, was institutionalized in a psychiatric facility. It is unknown as to how this finding was made as, with today's psychiatric knowledge, sociopathy or psychopathy on its own would certainly not be a determination for insanity in most countries in the world.

Personality disorders such as these cannot be treated or cured. Medication can help to lessen some of the pathologies that develop and psychotherapy can provide coping mechanisms, but institutionalizing a person living with a personality disorder would be completely unhelpful unless there were other pathologies present. Despite the fact that his sociopathy alone would not be a basis for insanity, just three years later, Pedro was declared "sane" and released. This is problematic because people living with sociopathic and psychopathic tendencies are often highly manipulative and are well-known for fooling even the most experienced of mental health professionals. It is for this reason that, today, in most countries, criminals with personality disorders are jailed, with access to psychotherapy and medication, and not institutionalized.

Pedro only had to pay a $50 parole fee to secure his release and there were a few additional stipulations to how he should behave on the outside as is standard with parole release. Sadly, there does not appear to have been any system in place to ensure that he was actually adhering to these conditions. His elderly mother would report that soon after his release, Pedro had arrived at her home demanding his inheritance. When he realized that the woman was living in poverty, he sold the only bed and chair she owned and pocketed the money.

In 2002, after being linked to a local murder, Pedro Lopez disappeared. To this day, the location of the "Monster of the Andes" is unknown (Biography.com editors, 2014).

While it is always difficult to determine why a serial killer does what he does, the sexual abuse that Pedro claimed to have suffered as a child may well have played into his eventual crimes. When fantasies of retribution are developing in an abused and simultaneously sociopathic mind, rather than wanting to gain revenge on the abuser, the killer may develop a fantasy of dominating the abused. In this case, Pedro may have chosen young girls because they both fulfilled his desire to dominate a child of the age he was when he was abused and those victims also may have fulfilled a sexual desire for him.

In both sociopathy and psychopathy, the person would find it impossible to have any empathy for their victim or their family, which is likely why Pedro continued unabated for so long.

Pedro Lopez earns his place in the top ten for a few reasons. His alleged victim count is, of course, horrendous on its own. The young age and vulnerable status of the victims he chose also stands out. Pedro did not just choose young children, he specifically chose children whose families would not have resources to search for their girls. This cold-blooded forethought certainly puts him in our countdown.

#9: Ted Bundy

The man's smile put her at ease. He seemed so vulnerable with his injured leg that surely there was no harm in helping him with whatever he needed from his car? The change came in seconds, though. So fast that she had no way of fighting back. One minute he was a kind, smiling, helpless man and then next, a monster from the depths of her nightmares.

The Early Days

Ted Bundy's mother, Louise, was just 22 and unmarried when she fell pregnant with her son. Ted's father would never be confirmed. Writer, Ann Rule, who would go on to pen a book about Ted's crimes, *The Stranger Beside Me*, would claim that his father was Lloyd Marshall, an air force veteran. Louise was also dating a man called Jack Worthington at the time, though, and a lewd rumor was claimed that Ted was the product of an incestuous rape of his mother by his grandfather.

In a time when having an illegitimate child was still deeply shameful, Louise's parents hid Ted's true identity by having her give birth at a home for unwed mothers far from their home in Philadelphia. After Ted's birth on November 24th, 1946, his grandparents passed him off as their adopted son and for the first few years of his life, Ted was told that his mother was actually his sister (Biography.com Editors, 2014).

A few years later, though, Louise left her parents' home and married Johnnie Bundy, taking Ted with her. It is believed that Ted had never really bonded with his stepfather. He felt that the man was uneducated and too working class for his mother and him, but Louise seemed happy with her husband and they would have several children together.

Despite his strange early start, his childhood with his mother and Johnnie appeared relatively normal and stable, but this did not stop Ted from displaying macabre interests from a very early age. By the age of three, he was already fascinated with knives, but he was also regarded as a bright child who excelled at school. From a social aspect, though, Ted was shy and did not get along with his peers.

As Bundy grew into a teenager, his darker side started to become more apparent. As is the case with many sexually-motivated serial killers, Bundy started out as a peeping tom. Occasionally the thrill from voyeurism was not enough and he would steal from people's homes without giving it a second thought.

Interestingly, Bundy would go on to graduate from the University of Washington with a degree in psychology. One could question whether this was an attempt at understanding the human mind from the perspective of someone who likely already realized he was very different from everyone else. Bundy clearly did not see a future for himself in psychology, though, and instead applied to law school in Utah to which he was accepted. He would never graduate with this degree.

While he was studying at the University of Washington, Bundy met and fell in love with a well-off, beautiful young woman from California. Bundy allegedly saw the woman as everything he deserved in a woman—money, class, and influence. When the girl broke up with him, Bundy was apparently devastated and it's alleged that his future victims looked very similar in appearance to this woman. By the mid-1970s, Bundy was very different from the shy and awkward teenager he had once been. He was outwardly confident and active in politics and social circles. After working on the campaign of the Republican governor of Washington, Bundy was even given a letter of recommendation for his excellent work.

This is not that surprising. Although we tend to see serial killers as these one-dimensional murderous beings, they really are just human beings with various aspects to their lives. One of those aspects happens to be serial murder, but this doesn't mean that they cannot be successful in business or have satisfactory relationships or marriages.

This was evident in that Bundy started a relationship with a woman named Elizabeth Kloepfer in 1969. The woman was a single mother of a young girl and struggled with alcoholism. She would later describe her relationship with Bundy as loving and warm and said that Bundy took very good care of her in the six years they were together (Biography.com Editors, 2014).

The Murders Begin

As with many serial killers, it is difficult to ascertain exactly when Bundy started killing. Many sources believe that his first kill was in 1974. It was around this time that women began to disappear in Seattle and Oregon. Rumors began to spread about how some of the women may have last been seen with a good-looking dark-haired man named Ted. It was alleged that many of the missing women had helped this man who had pretended to be injured. They had never been seen again. When the disappearances started in 1974, Bundy's girlfriend actually suspected that he was involved. She had found a meat cleaver in his drawer and he had started behaving very strangely. The woman reported her suspicions to police, who dismissed her claims.

In the fall of 1974, Ted Bundy started law school in Utah. This move coincided with a number of women going missing in that area. In 1975, a woman named Carol DaRonch was at a mall in Utah when a man claiming to be a police officer approached her. He told her that he had caught a man trying to break into her car and she needed to accompany him to the police station to complete a report. Carol felt unsure, but accompanied the man to his Volkswagen Beetle. She got in and the man immediately handcuffed her and attempted to hit her with a crowbar. Carol fought back and managed to escape. By the time police arrived, the man was gone.

Police took down Carol's statement with interest, as her description of the man's modus operandi and his appearance matched the many reports they had been receiving regarding missing women in Utah. There were also similar reports coming in from Washington and Colorado.

In August of that same year, Bundy was pulled over in a traffic stop and police found burglary tools, a face mask, rope, and handcuffs in his vehicle. He was arrested and Carol DaRonch identified him as the man that had attempted to abduct her. Ted Bundy was put on trial for this crime and convicted. He received a one-to-15-year jail sentence (Biography.com Editors, 2014).

While Bundy was in jail on this charge, he remained in contact with Elizabeth Kloepfer. On one phone call to her, he admitted that he had attempted to kill her in the past and that he could not control his murderous compulsions. Kloepfer once again went to police, but this time, with her evidence and their knowledge of the crime he had been convicted of, they believed her.

The Investigation and Convictions

With Bundy in jail, police continued to seek out evidence to link him to a string of disappearances and murders. In 1977, they indicted him on a murder charge in the death of a young Colorado woman. Bundy had opted to represent himself in this case and, as such, was given access to the courthouse library for preparation. During one trip, he jumped out of a window and escaped. He was recaptured eight days later.

Then in December of 1977, Bundy escaped again. It would later emerge that he had made a hole in the ceiling of his cell. In the weeks before the escape, Bundy had lost more than 30 pounds in weight and it is believed that he had done this in order to fit through the small opening. Although he should have been on tight watch considering his previous escape, Bundy was not missed for 15 hours, giving him an enormous head start on his pursuers.

Bundy would be on the run for almost three months this time. During this period, he broke into the Chi Omega Sorority house in Tallahassee, Florida and attacked four of the residents while they slept. Two of the women died. Bundy also abducted and murdered a 12-year-old girl named Kimberly Leach. He was pulled over in February, 1978 and returned to custody.

Police had found it difficult to connect many of the murders they suspected Bundy of to him conclusively, but his escape and the three murders he committed during that time, would be the proverbial (and literal) nail in his coffin.

With the murders being so recent, they were able to convict him of all three. The sorority house murders were linked to him predominantly using bite mark comparisons. He received a death sentence for each of the three murders.

Bundy would go on to appeal his sentence, even offering up information on some of the unsolved murders to avoid the electric chair.

It is widely acknowledged that Ted Bundy would rape his victims before killing them. He had also admitted to committing necrophilia with some of his victims. He confessed to having killed 36 women, decapitating 12 of those, but the FBI would later say that they believed he was responsible for more than 100 murders.

In February 1980, Bundy married a woman named Carol-Ann Boone. He had met Boone before his first arrest when they both worked in an emergency call room in Washington. Carol-Ann was a mother of two children and she and Bundy would have their own child together in 1982. At the time of this marriage, Carol-Ann had believed that Ted was innocent. After he started to confess to murders to escape the death penalty, she realized that he was in fact guilty and divorced him in 1986.

Bundy was executed in 1989. He requested that his ashes be scattered in the Cascade Mountains of Washington, an area in which he had murdered at least four of his victims (Biography.com Editors, 2014).

While Bundy's large number of alleged victims is horrifying on its own, he earns a place on this list for different reasons. Bundy's necrophilic abuse of his victim's corpses, although not unheard of with serial killers, is particularly shocking. Bundy truly was the epitome of a masked monster. He managed to continue on quite successfully in his day-to-day life. He achieved academically, did well in his jobs, and he was well-liked by those who knew him, but behind the wide smile and bubbly personality was the mind of a killer.

Although his murders appeared to coincide with the breakdown of the relationship with the college student, it is highly unlikely that this was the root cause of his desire to kill. Stressful situations, like the break up of a romantic relationship, are often catalysts for serial murderers to kill, but they are not the reasons. One note that stands out with Bundy is that he appears to have had a completely normal childhood. Certainly the initial situation with his grandparents pretending to be his parents was odd, but it would not likely have had much of an impact on him. The largest part of his childhood was spent in a middle-class living situation where no abuse was reported.

It certainly appears that Bundy was living with several personality disorders and would have ranked quite high on the psychopathy checklist. Even in his early years, he showed signs of delusions of grandeur and his admission that he felt absolutely nothing for his victims points to significant psychopathy.

Killers like Bundy are much more difficult to figure out than someone like Pedro Lopez. In Lopez's case, the sexual abuse he suffered helps us to understand how his fantasies may have developed, but with Bundy, this is less clear, and perhaps it is this very mystery that makes Ted Bundy one of our top ten most notorious serial killer of all time.

#8: Harold Shipman

The elderly lady sits back in her rocking chair and smiles at her doctor. She already feels better just knowing that he is at her side. She sees him rifling through some paperwork and wonders if he's going to ask her to sign something again like he did last time he was here. He sets the papers aside, though, and reaches into his medical bag, pulling out a syringe. The good doctor instructs her to lift her shirt sleeve and she does as she's told. The doctor knows best, after all. Soon darkness will envelop her, and the last face she sees will be that of the man who was supposed to heal her.

The Early Days

Harold Frederick Shipman was born into a working class family on January 14th, 1946 in Manchester, England. He was an intelligent child and he would later say that his interest in the medical field was sparked when, as a child, his mother developed terminal lung cancer and would regularly receive morphine injections to ease her pain.

He met his future wife, Primrose, when he was 19 and she was 17, and they married when she was five months pregnant with their first child.

He graduated with a medical degree from Leeds University in 1970 and within a few years, he was a popular general practitioner in Todmorden, Lancashire (Jenkins, 2019).

By 1975, Shipman had developed an addiction to the opiate pethedine. He was caught after having written several fraudulent prescriptions for the drug and he was forced out of his practice and given a small fine and a conviction on his record for forgery.

After having undergone drug rehabilitation, Shipman managed to find work as a general practitioner at Donneybrook Medical Center in Hyde, Greater Manchester. Here he managed to create a respectable image and his practice began to thrive. Despite his popularity with his patients, Shipman's coworkers did not enjoy working with the man, finding him arrogant and rude.

The Murders Begin

The local undertaker soon noticed that Harold Shipman's patients seemed to have an unusually high rate of death. There were also many similarities in the way shipman's patients died. They were all fully clothed and sitting upright or leaning back slightly on their couch or in a chair. The undertaker approached Shipman about this who, of course, assured him that there was no problem. A while later, another of

Shipman's colleagues, Dr. Susan Booth, also became concerned with the huge number of patients Shipman was losing and she alerted the local coroner's office, who, in turn, alerted the police (Jenkins, 2019).

The Investigation and Conviction

After Dr. Booth's allegations came to light, police conducted a covert investigation which initially cleared him of any wrongdoing. Unfortunately, the investigation was carried out rather half-heartedly and investigators failed to check Shipman's previous criminal record or contact the General Medical Council. Had this been done, Shipman's penchant for forgery would have been uncovered and his records, which appeared to clear him on the surface, would have been more thoroughly examined.

A later investigation would prove that Shipman had altered his patient's medical records in order to corroborate the causes of death that he had preferred.

Although it is difficult to determine exactly when Shipman started his murder series, it would be one particular murder that would put an end to his run of carnage. In 1998, 81-year-old Kathleen Grundy was discovered dead in her home just hours after Dr. Shipman had visited. Her family was shocked at the woman's sudden death as she had been in good health and lived an active life. They became further perplexed when they noted that her will had been changed. It now benefited her doctor, Harold Shipman, and her entire estate (valued at about £400,000) had been left to him. The doctor also insisted that no autopsy was necessary. Unfortunately for Shipman, Grundy's daughter, Angela Woodruff, was a lawyer and she had always handled her mother's affairs, so she immediately knew that this new will had to be a forgery. She also suspected that Harold Shipman had murdered her mother (Biography.com Editors, 2017).

Woodruff alerted local police and after an investigation, they came to the same conclusion.

Grundy's body was exhumed and it was determined that she had died of a morphine overdose which had been administered within three hours of her death. This put the time of the overdose being administered within the same time frame that Dr. Shipman had visited Grundy. A search warrant was obtained for Shipman's home and police seized medical records, a mismatched collection of jewelry, and an old typewriter. Analysts were able to determine that Grundy's forged will had been typed on this very typewriter.

The medical records recovered from Shipman's home indicated that the police were looking at far more than one murder. Given the enormous scope of the investigation, priority was given to cases in which evidence would be available. These would include those deceased patients who had been buried rather than cremated and also those who had been seen by Shipman in the hours before their death.

Shipman had not only suggested to his patients' families that autopsies were not necessary, but he had also encouraged most of them to cremate their family members rather than bury them. This meant that many of Shipman's murders would go unproven.

Although Shipman had gone to the trouble of altering each of his patient's records to match the cause of death he would later pronounce, he did not realize that the computer system time-stamped these changes so it was easy enough for police to determine which records had been altered.

After an extensive investigation, on September 7th, 1998, Harold Shipman was charged with 15 counts of murder and one count of forgery (Biography.com Editors, 2017).

Shipman's trial started in Preston Crown Court more than a year later and the prosecution's case was that he had killed his patients because he enjoyed the control. Shipman's defence was that any deaths which may have been attributed to his actions were acts of compassion. This defence was dismissed because none of Shipman's victims had been suffering from a terminal illness.

Some of the most compelling evidence in the trial included Angela Woodruff's testimony, the pathologist's testimony regarding the morphine toxicity found in almost all the exhumed bodies, the fingerprint analysis of Grundy's will showing that the woman had never handled the document, and the computer analysis of the amended records.

Further witnesses in the trial also produced proof of another cold-blooded behavior by Shipman. On request of panicked family members, he would pretend to call emergency services and further pretend to cancel those services when he pronounced the patient dead, but telephone records showed that he had never phoned emergency services for any of his patients.

Shipman was also found to have been hoarding drugs, including morphine.

On January 31st, 2000, a jury found Harold Shipman guilty of all the charges against him. The judge handed down 15 life sentences plus four years for the forgery charge. This was commuted to a whole life tariff which in British law means that Shipman will never leave prison.

It is believed that Harold Shipman was active as a serial killer for about 24 months and he may have been guilty of killing at least 236 of his patients (Biography.com Editors, 2017).

Despite the significant evidence against him, Shipman maintained his innocence and his wife and family continued to stand by him throughout his trial and incarceration. On January 13th, 2004, Harold Shipman was found hanging from the bars of his cell with bed sheets wrapped around his neck. While his death was considered a suicide, his family believe he was murdered.

Harold Shipman had a huge victim count, but it is the position that he held at the time of his murders that earns the man a spot in our top ten list. As a doctor, he not only had a duty of care and to "first, do no harm" but he also had significant power over the patients which he abused. We tend to accept that medical professionals know the correct course of action when it comes to our health and, for the most part, we don't question their advice or treatment. The group of people that Shipman chose to target came from a generation who would definitely not have questioned a doctor and they would likely not even have asked what he was injecting into their arms.

It is entirely possible that Shipman's childhood experience of watching his mother die of lung cancer and receive morphine injections helped to form his fantasy around killing. Over time, this fantasy likely developed into a power and control addiction and added to that was the benefit of gaining financial benefit through faking wills and stealing items of value from his victims' homes.

Sadly, it is not uncommon to find serial murderers in the medical profession and among female serial murderers, three quarters of the most prolific killers were nurses. This of course begs the question—do these people go into the medical profession in order to have access to victims or is it simply a horrifying coincidence?

#7: John Wayne Gacy

The clown's face is drawn into a permanent bright red smile. His antics make the crowd squeal with joy and children's parties are his domain. It is not this happy face that his after-hours visitors see, though. Young men arrive at the clown's home and they never leave. The house that should be filled with joy is a growing graveyard.

The Early Days

John Wayne Gacy was born on March 17th, 1942 in Chicago, Illinois. His parents were Danish and Polish and his father was an abusive alcoholic who beat Gacy, as well as all of his siblings and their mother. Gacy's sister would confirm this abuse and said that her brother and all of his siblings learned to harden themselves against the beatings and not to cry.

Gacy was born with a congenital heart defect and this meant that he was further isolated as he was unable to play with other children. His father also saw this as a failing on his part. As Gacy aged into his teenage years and realized that he was attracted to men, he experienced great emotional turmoil.

Despite this tumultuous early start, Gacy grew into a popular and at least outwardly successful adult. During the 1960s, he worked as a manager in the fast food industry and then started his own building contracting business. In the 1970s, he was the Democratic precinct captain in the suburbs of Chicago.

Gacy was well-liked and respected within his community. He married and divorced twice and had two biological children and two stepchildren.

Gacy's role as a clown stemmed from his membership in the Jolly Joker Clown Club. He often performed in full clown attire at fundraisers and children's parties under the stage names "Pogo the Clown," or "Patches the Clown."

Gacy's first brush with the law came in 1968 when two teenage boys accused him of sexually assaulting them. He was convicted and given 10 years in prison. Sadly, he was released on parole after serving just two years of his sentence. In 1971, he was rearrested after another sexual assault accusation, but that charge was dropped when the victim did not arrive to testify.

As is the case with serial rapists, Gacy's imprisonment for his crimes did not serve to correct his behavior. Rather, he simply decided that from that point on, he would leave no victim behind to testify against him (Biography.com, 2017).

The Murders Begin

John Wayne Gacy's first known victim was 16-year-old Timothy McCoy. Gacy would use various ploys to lure young boys to his home. Most often, he offered them construction work.

By the mid-1970s, two more young men accused Gacy of sexual assault, bringing him to the police's attention once again. He was also questioned about a string of disappearances where the victims matched the profile of his rape and sexual assault victims.

By the time 15-year-old Robert Piest went missing on the 11th of December, 1978, Gacy had been killing for at least six years. Robert's mother told police that her son had been headed to Gacy's house to discuss a potential job in construction.

Investigation and Conviction

With Gacy's background and him now being the last known person to have seen a missing boy, police gained a search warrant for his home in Norwood Park, Illinois. They uncovered several trenches under his home filled with human remains. Gacy confessed to killing 30 young men. He would be conclusively linked to another three murders and suspected of several more (Biography.com, 2017).

The house, located on Summerdale Avenue in Norwood Park, not far from O'Hare International Airport, had come to the attention of neighbors on a few occasions before Gacy was arrested due to a bad odor emanating from the premises. Gacy would excuse the smell by saying it was caused by rodents or mold.

Gacy had used his construction skills to build a trapdoor in the home which led to the crawl space underneath the home. This is where many of his victims were found. Some were also found in his backyard and still others were dumped in the nearby Des Plaines River.

Gacy was not able to identify all of his victims and after significant investigation, there remained eight bodies that could not be identified.

Gacy's house would eventually be completely dismantled and demolished to ensure that police had found all of the victims' remains.

Gacy's trial began on the 6th of February, 1980. As he had already confessed to the murders, the main focus of the trial was to determine whether Gacy could be found liable for his crimes from a mental health perspective. He was sent for a term of mental health evaluation so that the court could understand whether his claims of having an alternate personality had any basis. During the trial, mental health experts testified both for the prosecution and the defence. Gacy would eventually be found guilty of 33 murders. He was handed down 12 death sentences, as well as 21 natural life sentences.

Despite his confessions, Gacy would launch multiple appeals for almost 15 years after his initial conviction. During this time, he was incarcerated in Menard Correctional Center where he took up studying visual arts. His paintings would later be exhibited at a gallery in Chicago.

When all of Gacy's appeals were unsuccessful, he was transferred to death row at Stateville Correctional Center and executed by lethal injection on the 10th of May 1994.

In 2017, one of those identified victims got his name back when the so-called "Victim No. 24" was identified through DNA as James Byron Haakenson. In the same year, Mullock's Auctions in Shropshire, UK auctioned off several pieces of Gacy's art as well as framed crime scene photographs from the excavation of his house (Biography.com, 2017).

Despite Gacy's protestations of innocence, the fact remains that the bodies of several young men were found under his home and those young men went missing while he lived at the property. Gacy's difficult home life as a child could certainly have played into his crimes, but it certainly would not be an overriding reason. Gacy earns his space on this list for two reasons. Firstly, he was a true predator. He lured young men to his home under false pretences. These victims were just trying to get construction work and make their lives better and he took advantage of that. The second thing that makes Gacy one of the worst serial killers of all time is the clown component.

While providing his confessions to police Gacy notoriously said, "A clown can get away with murder." Gacy used this symbol of fun and delight and twisted it into something evil and terrifying.

#6: Charles Sobraj

The young woman throws her head back as she laughs. She's bikini-clad and enjoying a holiday in paradise. She hasn't a care in the world and certainly has no idea that a predator is watching her. Soon, she'll become his victim and part of one of the strangest stories ever told.

The Early Days

Hotchand Bhawnani Gurumukh Charles Sobhraj was born in Saigon, Vietnam, on April 6th, 1944 to a Vietnamese mother and an Indian father. He is alleged to have spent a significant amount of time living on the streets as a child and being passed off between his mother and father. His mother would later marry a soldier in the French army and have another child with the man. Sobhraj was initially not accepted by his stepfather, but he would later accompany his mother and her new family to France.

As a teenager, Sobhraj committed a string of petty crimes and was first imprisoned in 1963. While in prison, he allegedly manipulated prison guards to grant him special favors. Sobhraj's charming nature meant that he was able to endear himself to many and while serving his first prison sentence, he met and befriended a prison volunteer named Felix d'Escogne. Felix was very wealthy and when Sobhraj left prison, he moved in with the man who introduced him to the high society circles of Paris. Sobhraj did not intend to leave his criminal past behind him though and fluidly moved between the rich and famous of France and the criminal underworld. During his time in Felix's circles, Sobhraj met a young French woman named Chantal Compagnon. The girl was from a well-to-do and conservative family but she fell deeply in love with Sobhraj. He seemed rather enamored with her, too, although it's likely she was more of a meal ticket to him than a life partner. Regardless of his motives, just a single day after proposing marriage to Chantal, Sobhraj was arrested for car theft.

After his release, he married Chantal and they had a child together. The couple would travel across Afghanistan and India, leaving a string of robbery victims behind until Chantal decided she'd had enough and left Sobhraj, returning to France.

After this, Sobhraj then committed another string of identity theft scams and robberies with his half-brother, Andre. When one heist went wrong, Sobhraj left his brother behind and the young man was arrested and sentenced to 18 years in prison.

Sobhraj then became involved in a relationship with a woman named Marie-Andree Leclerc. The woman would become both his lover and his partner in crime (Biography.com, 2014). He also worked with an Indian man named Ajay Chowdbury.

The Murders Begin

Sobhraj would go on to travel across several countries committing robberies and later, murders. His initial murders are believed to have occurred in the 1970s when he operated across Asia befriending, drugging, robbing, and killing mainly Western tourists. He is believed to have killed between 12 and 24 people between 1972 and 1976.

Sobhraj did not operate in the same way that most serial killers do, in that he did not stick to a specific geographical area. Much like Pedro Alonso, he remained undetected for a long time by constantly moving to different countries. He is even alleged to have escaped custody in four different countries.

Another aspect of Sobhraj's modus operandi that made him difficult to catch was the fact that he was a skilled con artist and he was fluent in several languages. Sobhraj was essentially a human chameleon, blending into his surroundings no matter where he went, until he found the victim he wanted, and then he would pounce.

Many of Sobhraj's murders were committed in an area known as the "Hippie Trail." This is a stretch of land that runs between Afghanistan, Nepal, and Southeast Asia. Here, he would prey on young backpackers in crimes that earned him nicknames such as "The Bikini Killer" (in reference to the swimsuit one of his victims had been wearing) and "The Serpent" (as he always seemed to slither out of reach of the authorities.)

Investigation and Conviction

Sobhraj was able to continue killing individuals for a long period of time without being apprehended, but in 1976, he chose to up the ante in India and attempted to drug an entire group of tourists. A few of the victims managed to fight the effects of the drug for long enough to call for help and Sobhraj was arrested.

The Thai government want Sobhraj extradited to Thailand to face murder charges there, but the Indian government insisted on trying Sobhraj and Leclerc for the murder of an Israeli tourist first. He was given a sentence of seven years in jail in India after which, Indian authorities said they would send him to Thailand to face charges there (Biography.com, 2014).

In 1986, though, Sobhraj and a group of other inmates escaped after drugging guards during a party on the prison grounds. He was captured less than a month after his escape, but with the additional prison time he was given for the escape, by the time Sobhraj had completed his sentence in India, the statute of limitations had run out on his crimes in Thailand.

With no other immediate charges to answer to, Sobhraj was released and he returned to France. However, his freedom would not last long as he was arrested in Nepal in 2003 for the murders of two backpackers that dated back to 1975. He attempted to escape from prison in 2004, but that attempt failed.

Perhaps one of the most terrifying things about Charles Sobhraj was his ability to fool the people he came into contact with. His victims were all tourists and being in holiday mode, would likely have had their guard down. They were easy targets, but also the types of victims whose murders would garner great media and police attention. Despite this, Sobhraj saw fit to target these people and, at least initially, easily escaped capture by continuously moving around.

Another aspect of Sobhraj's crimes that earn him a spot on our top ten list is the fact that he so deeply conned most of his victims. Sobhraj would often drug victims to convince them they were ill, and then help "nurse" them back to health, thereby gaining their trust. In this way, he would extort as much money as he could out of his victims before killing them.

Although Sobhraj's childhood was far from ideal, he appears to have been a born criminal and his early stints in prison only served to hone his skills.

#5: Jack the Ripper

The young woman gathers her coat around her against the chill of the English winter night. Several street lamps are not working and shadows lurk ominously around every corner. She's close to her room, though, just a few more steps and she'll be safe for the night. The Ripper will take her before then though.

The Crimes

This serial killer is a little different from the others on our list as we do not have a name for him. The man that terrorized London, England in 1888, killing at least five women, has never been positively identified. To this day, his name remains synonymous with terror and mystery.

All five of the murders that would be attributed to Jack the Ripper took place within a mile of each other. These murders occurred within the Whitechapel district of London's East End and happened in a single month from the 7th of August to the 10th of September, 1888.

The five victims in this part of the series were all believed to be sex workers and included: Mary Ann Nichols, Elizabeth Stride, Catherine Eddowes, Mary Jane Kelly, and Annie Chapman. At the time of their murders, all but one were working the streets (History.com Editors, 2018).

London's West End in the late 1800s was a place where immigrants often arrived to start their new lives. It also became a place filled with violence, crime, and abject poverty. Around this time, sex work was only viewed as an issue by the police if it caused a public disturbance, but sex workers were viewed as second-class citizens. If a sex worker was murdered or found dead, there was hardly any mention of it. It was therefore not uncommon for sex workers to be beaten to death by the men procuring their services. When the Whitechapel murders began, that would later be ascribed to Jack the Ripper, they stood in stark contrast to the individual murders that had become rather commonplace. The sadistic butchery involved in the crimes, including mutilation, disembowelment, and the removal of organs, was something the residents of Whitechapel had never seen before. It appeared that the killer held a deep hatred for women in general. The method of mutilation also seemed to point to the killer having some knowledge of human anatomy.

Several other murders were committed around the same time, but these were investigated as a separate series of crimes.

In the days after the murders, London police started to receive letters which were allegedly from the killer. The letters taunted investigators, promised more murders, and also gave rise to the moniker, Jack the Ripper. One letter contained a gruesome accompaniment: a piece of a human kidney (History.com Editors, 2018).

The Theories

Over the years, several theories have developed about the killer's identity. Among these were claims that the Ripper was a famous Victorian painter, Walter Sickert, and even Queen Victoria's grandson. More than 100 suspects have been identified since 1888 and this has only served to stoke the fires of this mystery.

In 2011, British detective Trevor Marriott was denied access to uncensored documents regarding the Whitechapel murders by London police. Marriott had dedicated much of his life to investigating the Ripper crimes and believed that the answers lay in those documents. The police, however, said that providing him with the documents could reveal the identity of police informants and impede the possibility of future testimony by individuals with information around the case.

In 2014, amateur sleuth and author Russell Edwards announced that he believed he had identified Jack the Ripper. The identification was allegedly made by using DNA evidence found in the modern day on a piece of clothing from one of the victims. Edwards claimed that the DNA matched a known suspect at the time of the murders— Polish immigrant Aaron Kosminski (History.com Editors, 2018).

Five years later, two biochemists believed to have found evidence to support Kominski's guilt when tests they conducted also matched the man's DNA. Geneticists, though, challenged the claim saying that the methodology used was errant and the piece of clothing from the victim may have been contaminated over the years.

It is likely that this case has maintained its hold on the public's imagination over such a long period of time because instances of serial murder were rather rare in the 1800s.

Jack the Ripper makes our list of top ten serial killers because of the brutality of his crimes during a time when the act of serial murder was relatively rare and heavy mutilation was almost unheard of. Of course, his enduring anonymity also ramps up his infamy levels and we can't help but wonder where the Ripper may have gone after the Whitechapel murders ended.

Today we know that serial killers rarely stop killing until they are caught, so it is postulated that the Ripper must have either died, been imprisoned for a very long period, or moved somewhere else and carried on killing there. For the most part, serial killers will start killing in their mid-twenties to early-thirties. If the Ripper was around this age in 1888, and he moved areas and continued killing somewhere else with a slightly different modus operandi, he may well have committed his crimes all the way up to the 1930s. Of course, at that time travel was not tracked as well as it is today and the Ripper could have moved anywhere in the world and simply carried on killing.

#4: Jeffrey Dahmer

The young man is out on the town for a night of fun. When the attractive blonde man catches his eye and they start talking he thinks his night is made. By the time he realizes that something is very wrong he is already back at the man's home and it is far too late.

The Early Days

Jeffrey Dahmer was born to Lionel and Joyce Dahmer in Milwaukee, Wisconsin on May 21st, 1960. His parents would describe him as initially being a happy child and full of energy, but a surgery he had to undergo when he was four years old would change his demeanor significantly. The surgery was for a double hernia and his recovery period coincided with the birth of his younger brother. These circumstances paired with the fact that his family moved regularly, seemed to have a major impact on Jeffrey's personality. By the time he reached his teens, he was tense, disengaged, and, for the most part, friendless.

Dahmer would later say that by the age of 14, he was already experiencing compulsions around murder and necrophilia. He believed that the breakdown of his parents' marriage was the catalyst for him turning these compulsions into actions.

Dahmer began to self-medicate with alcohol and when his drinking caused him to drop out of his courses at Ohio State University, his father demanded that he join the army. It is very likely that Lionel Dahmer believed that the army would be a good influence on his son, but this is not what happened. Dahmer enlisted in December 1978 and was sent to Germany. His drinking continued and by 1981 he had been discharged by the army for his conduct (Biography.com Editors, 2017).

It would later emerge that by the time Dahmer enlisted in the army, he had already begun killing.

The Murders Begin

Jeffrey Dahmer would later admit that his increased alcohol consumption and his leaving university coincided with his first murder. He picked up a hitchhiker named Steven Hicks and took him back to his parents' home. He then proceeded to get Hicks drunk and when he tried to leave, Dahmer killed him by hitting him in the head with a barbell and then strangled him. Dahmer then dismembered Hicks' body and buried the body parts in plastic bags on his parents' property. He would later dig the parts up, crush the bones with a sledgehammer, and scatter them across a wooded ravine. It is highly unusual for a killer to dismember their very first victim, as this is usually behavior that only comes later in a series of crimes. For

Dahmer, though, dismemberment was already part of his fantasy.

Although German authorities would later investigate the possibility that Dahmer had killed while in the army in their country, the general consensus is that he did not take any more victims while enlisted.

After being discharged from the army, Dahmer returned to Ohio. He was arrested for disorderly conduct in the same year and his father sent him to live with his grandmother in Wisconsin. Dahmer's behavior did not improve there and he was arrested again for indecent exposure. Then, in 1986, two boys accused Dahmer of masturbating in front of them and he was convicted and received a one-year probationary sentence.

Unfortunately, we now understand that this type of behavior is very often a precursor to more serious offences. Serial rapists and murderers will often start with "peeping Tom" type behavior and indecent exposure. When these acts are not taken seriously enough and sentences do not include mandatory mental health treatment, these offenders will almost always escalate their behavior once they are free. For Dahmer, these acts he was caught for were actually red flags that he was already committing other, more serious crimes, and because he was not looked at more carefully, he continued.

Between 1978 and 1991, Jeffrey Dahmer would murder 17 men. He carefully selected his victims ensuring that the men he took were on the fringes of society and would not necessarily be looked for immediately. This is also a familiar refrain for many serial killers. It is not that these victims necessarily fit their ideal victim mold, but they know if they select more high profile victims, they are likely to be caught much sooner.

After an almost nine-year gap, Dahmer killed his second victim. Dahmer met Steven Tuomi and invited him to a hotel room. They drank and Dahmer claims that he woke up to find Tuomi dead and he had no memory of what had happened the previous night. Dahmer transported Tuomi's body to his grandmother's basement in a large suitcase where he dismembered him, masturbated with the corpse, and then disposed of the remains.

Dahmer would kill another two victims at his grandmother's house before she became annoyed with what she saw as his late night drunken activities and asked him to leave in 1988.

The following year, Dahmer had a very lucky escape when he raped a 13-year-old boy and was charged with sexual exploitation and second-degree sexual assault. Dahmer pleaded guilty. He was released on bail while awaiting sentencing for this crime and, while out on bail, he lured Anthony Sears to his grandmother's home and drugged, strangled, sodomized, photographed, dismembered, and disposed of his remains.

During Dahmer's trial for the molestation charges, he was presented as eloquent and contrite. He told the court that he could see exactly what he had done wrong and this would be a turning point in his life. His defence attorney asked that Dahmer be given mental health treatment and not a prison sentence. The judge agreed and gave Dahmer a one-year sentence with day release conditions. He was allowed to work during the day and had to return to prison at night. He was also given a five-year suspended sentence.

Several years later, Lionel Dahmer would tell the media that he had written a letter to the court asking that they mandate psychiatric treatment before his release. Unfortunately, this request was ignored and Dahmer was released from his sentence after serving 10 months.

Dahmer lived with his grandmother briefly after his release and then moved into his own apartment. This independence and having his own space seriously accelerated Dahmer's murder rate. He would go from four victims to 17 in just two years. As he progressed, he would develop rituals and he would also start to experiment with chemical means of body disposal. He also began to cannibalize the flesh of some of his victims.

Dahmer performed some horrific experiments on his victims including crude lobotomy-like operations and drilling into the victim's skulls while they were still alive and then injecting muriatic acid into the drilled hole.

On May 27th, 1991, a neighbor of Dahmer's called the police to report that there was a young boy running naked down the road. When police arrived, instead of providing assistance to the naked child (the boy was only 14 years old), they took Dahmer's word that this was just a lover's spat and the young man was actually his 19-year-old lover. Police did not want to become involved in what they viewed as a homosexual domestic incident and they returned the boy to Dahmer's apartment. It would emerge that the boy, who Dahmer promptly killed shortly after police left, was the brother of the boy he had been found guilty of molesting a few years before (Biography.com Editors, 2017).

Police did not make any effort to look around Dahmer's apartment when they returned the boy. If they had, they would have found the body of Dahmer's 12th victim.

Investigation and Conviction

On July 22nd, 1991, Jeffrey Dahmer's killing spree came to an end when two Milwaukee police officers picked a 32-year-old man named Tracy Edwards who was found wandering the streets with a set of handcuffs hanging from his wrist. Edwards claimed that he had been drugged and restrained by a man. Thankfully, the police officers decided to investigate his claims and Edwards took them back to Dahmer's apartment. When they arrived, Dahmer very calmly offered to get the keys for the handcuffs. Dahmer likely thought that he would be able to use the same explanation that he had with his previous victim that had escaped, but this time police weren't leaving without seeing the bedroom Edwards said he had been restrained in. There, they discovered photographs of dismembered bodies and immediately placed Dahmer under arrest.

Additional searches revealed body parts in Dahmer's refrigerator, preserved body parts in jars, and an enormous collection of photographs of his victims in various stages of dismemberment.

Dahmer stood trial in Milwaukee in 1992. Despite having initially confessed to all the murders and pleading guilty, Dahmer would eventually change his plea to guilty by virtue of insanity.

In February 1992, Jeffrey Dahmer was found guilty, but sane, on all charges against him. He was sentenced to 16 consecutive life terms.

Dahmer was initially kept away from other prisoners, but he eventually requested to be allowed to integrate with the general population. This would end up being his undoing when on November 28th, 1994, Dahmer, and another man, were beaten to death by a fellow inmate (Biography.com Editors, 2017).

Jeffrey Dahmer would claim many different reasons for his crimes. Chief among these being loneliness and that when the men he brought to his home wanted to leave, he lost his temper and ensured that they would never leave. This excuse seems rather unbelievable considering the fact that the men that survived his attacks would say that he had drugged them almost immediately upon their arrival at his apartment.

The reason for Jeffrey Dahmer's inclusion in the list is most definitely the heinous nature of his crimes. The torture, dismemberment, horrific experiments, and cannibalism which formed part of his crimes make Dahmer one of the most vicious and horrific serial killers of his time.

#3: H.H. Holmes

The man enters the door to the hotel. He's grateful to have found accommodation on such short notice so he pushes down the strange feeling in his gut. Something is not quite right about this place and its owner. As he hears a lock click behind him, he realizes too late that he has made a grave mistake.

The Early Days

The man who would become known by his pseudonym H.H. Holmes was born Herman Webster Mudgett on May 16th, 1861 in Gilmanton, New Hampshire. Holmes was born into a wealthy family and is said to have been extremely intelligent, even as a child.

Holmes expressed an interest in studying medicine early on and this seemed to give him the excuse to "practice" by dissecting animals. Some sources allege that Holmes may have been responsible for the death of a school friend in his youth.

Despite wanting for nothing during his childhood, he started his life of crime very early with scams and fraud. While studying medicine at the University of Michigan, he stole corpses and used them to lodge fake insurance claims.

In 1885, Holmes moved to Chicago and started working in a pharmacy. It was at this time that he started using the pseudonym Dr. Henry H. Holmes. He would eventually take over this business and it was alleged that he had killed the owner in order to do so.

While working at this pharmacy, Holmes had a three-storey building constructed nearby which he would turn into his very own house of horrors. Holmes lived in the upper levels of the home and these levels also contained a room where he would torture and kill his victims. He had trapdoors and chutes installed that he used to move bodies down to the basement, where he would usually burn the remains in a kiln (Biography.com Editors, 2021).

The Murders Begin

Holmes' murders began in earnest during the 1893 Columbian Exposition. This was a fair that was held in Chicago to celebrate the 400th anniversary of Christopher Columbus' discovery of the New World. The fair drew visitors from all over the world and it brought a significant economic boom to Chicago. Many property owners opened up their homes to visitors as accommodation and Holmes turned his large home into a hotel.

His motive in doing this was not to make some money off the fair like everyone else. Holmes was keen to get these people into his home as they would be sitting ducks as victims. Many guests would stay in what has since been termed Holmes' "Murder Castle" during the Exposition, but very few would leave. While the exact number of victims Holmes took during that time has never been determined, mostly female victims would be seduced, conned, and then killed by Holmes. The man was well-known for becoming engaged to young women only for his fiancée to mysteriously disappear.

When the World Fair came to an end, Holmes left Chicago and became involved with a plan to fake the death of an associate, Benjamin Pitezel, and collect on his insurance. Holmes, however, had no intention of faking the man's death and thought the scheme would go off far smoother if Pitezel was really dead. He would also not have to share the life insurance claim with anyone.

Holmes would prove his absolute cold-blooded nature when Pitezel's widow began enquiring after his whereabouts. The woman, of course, still believed that her husband's death had been faked and Holmes let her believe this, convincing her, and three of her children, to accompany him to Pitezel's location. Instead, Holmes murdered the woman and the children. They would be his final victims.

Investigation and Conviction

Shortly after killing the Pitezel family, Holmes was apprehended by authorities and taken into custody. While in custody, Holmes provided a variety of stories to police about his crimes, at one point claiming that he had killed 27 people. The estimates as to Holmes' victims vary between 20 to 200.

He was convicted of the Pitezel murders in 1895 and despite appealing, he lost and was hanged in 1986 (Biography.com Editors, 2021).

The infamy of H.H. Holmes is multifaceted. He was one of the first convicted serial killers in the United States. The fact that he carefully designed a house to carry out his murders is a chilling detail that cannot be ignored. Finally, the fact is that we will never truly know exactly how many people Holmes killed and most of those victims will never be identified nor receive the justice they deserve.

#2: Richard Ramirez

The woman hears a strange sound in the middle of the night. Her eyes fly open immediately, but it takes some time for her vision to adjust to the thick darkness of her bedroom. For a moment she wonders if the sound was her neighbors moving around in their apartment, but then her eyes begin to adjust and she sees the shadow of a man moving toward her.

The Early Days

Ricardo Leyva Munoz Ramirez, who went by Richard, was born on February 29th, 1960 to Mexican immigrant parents. Richard was one of five children and grew up in El Paso, Texas.

Ramirez would develop epilepsy as a child after he was knocked unconscious by a swing on a playground. He also started using drugs quite early in life.

It's alleged that Ramirez's older cousin, Miguel, was a major formative influence in his life as a child. The man was a Vietnam War veteran and he allegedly showed photographs to a 12-year-old Richard of women he had raped, tortured, and killed during the war in Vietnam. Miguel and Richard smoked marijuana together. When Richard was 13, he would witness Miguel fatally shoot his wife.

In his early teens, Ramirez began to break into homes. He dropped out of high school in the ninth grade and was arrested for the first time in 1977 for marijuana possession. After this, he moved to Los Angeles where he continued to commit crimes and became addicted to cocaine. He would be arrested twice and briefly imprisoned in 1981 and 1984 for stealing a car.

The Murders Begin

Ramirez's home invasions soon turned to rape and murder and his first confirmed murder was that of 79-year-old Jennie Vincow, who he raped and stabbed to death after breaking into her house. This crime occurred in June 1984. It would later be determined, however, that Ramirez may well have started killing before this. Although he would never be convicted of the crime in question, Ramirez's DNA would show up at a crime scene where a 9-year-old girl was murdered in April 1984. There was no reason for the man's DNA to be at the crime scene and it is therefore highly likely that this was his first murder (The Editors of Encyclopedia Britannica, 2019).

On March 17th, 1985, Ramirez attacked Maria Hernandez and her roommate Dayle Okazaki. Maria managed to escape while Dayle was murdered. On the very same night, Ramirez killed Tsai-Lian Yu in another home invasion.

On March 27th, 1985, Ramirez murdered Vincent and Maxine Zazzara. In this crime he used the modus operandi that would become common for him. He would first shoot the male of the couple and then went on to brutally assault and stab to death the female. In this instance, he also gouged out Maxine's eyes.

Despite a full-scale police operation, Ramirez was able to commit another, almost identical attack, on William and Lillie Doi in May of 1985. At this point, Ramirez's crimes escalated considerably and he would target another 12 victims in just a few months.

Most of Ramirez's crimes took place in the Los Angeles area and his victims would be beaten, sexually assaulted, and often strange symbols were left at the scene.

When the public began to realize that there was a serial killer on the loose, gun sales soared, and the media dubbed the killer, "The Night Stalker." This relentless media and police pressure eventually caused Ramirez to leave the Los Angeles area. He arrived in San Francisco on August 17th, 1985 and took two more victims there—Peter and Barbara Pan (Biography.com Editors, 2017b).

Ramirez's final night of crime would occur on August 24th, 1985 when he was spotted outside a home in Mission Viejo. He had left a footprint behind and a witness was able to remember his vehicle license plate. Later that night, he raped another woman and shot her fiancé. Both survived and the woman was able to provide a detailed description of her assailant to police.

Investigation and Conviction

A few days after this final night of terror, police found Ramirez's abandoned car and it would be a single fingerprint left behind in the vehicle that would result in the identification of Richard Ramirez as "The Night Stalker". Ramirez's fingerprints were in the Automated Fingerprint Identification System (AFIS) after his arrests for several petty crimes and when the print from the crime scene was run through the system, Ramirez's name came up.

On August 30th, 1985, Ramirez's name and photograph were published by the media. The next day, a member of the public spotted Ramirez in East Los Angeles and called police. A chase ensued and Ramirez attempted to steal a car, but he was surrounded by a crowd and beaten until police arrived to arrest him.

Ramirez claimed to be a devil worshipper and made several references to this throughout his trial which began in early 1989.

The trial would become something of a spectacle with the man developing a cult-like following of people who attended his trial dressed all in black. There would be several delays in this trial with one juror being found murdered on the 14th of August 1989. There would be rumors that Ramirez had orchestrated the woman's murder from his jail cell, but these claims were found to be untrue.

In September 1989, Ramirez was convicted of 13 murders as well as a range of other crimes. When he was sentenced to death he was recorded as saying, "Big deal. Death always went with the territory. I'll see you in Disneyland."

Ramirez was suspected of several other rapes and murders but was never charged with these other crimes.

While incarcerated and appealing his conviction, in 1996, Ramirez would marry one of his supporters, 41-year-old, Doreen Lioy. His appeal would be rejected in 2006 (Biography.com Editors, 2017b).

In 2013, while on death row at San Quentin State prison, Ramirez was diagnosed with cancer and at the age of 53, died that same year (The Editors of Encyclopedia Britannica, 2019).

Richard Ramirez is one of the most feared serial killers in history and this likely has much to do with the legend he created for himself. Ramirez's crimes coincided with a time in the US which is now known as the "Satanic panic." During this period, the public and many members of law enforcement became convinced that devil worshipping cults were on the prowl and committing savage murders. This belief became so entrenched in society at this time that when Ramirez claimed to be committing these vicious crimes on the bequest of the devil himself, the fear level would only have increased.

In the mid-1990s, religious experts and law enforcement began to accept that many murderers were simply using various occult practices in what they thought would be a get-out-of-jail-free card. The vicious murders that Richard Ramirez committed were not in any way linked to any form of religious or occult practice. Whatever ideas the man had formed in his own head were simply the result of a depraved mind.

Looking back at Ramirez's childhood, it is clear that he was exposed to horrific levels of violence very early on. This could only have helped to shape his thinking. His head injury as a child and also his drug use while his brain was still forming may also have played a part in the development of abnormal thinking patterns.

Richard Ramirez earns his place on our top ten list not just because of the levels of fear he instilled in the people of Los Angeles and San Francisco, but also because he seemed to revel in that fear.

#1: Ed Gein

Through the thick black curtain of night that shrouds the graveyard, the shape of a figure moving among the headstones can just be made out. The superstitious may believe it to be a ghost, the restless spirit of a long-dead resident, but the reality is far more frightening. The man has come to the graveyard not to pay his respects or leave flowers, but to take the remains of those laid to rest to add to his collection.

The Early Days

Edward Theodore Gein was born on August 27th, 1906 in La Crosse, Wisconsin. Gein had a difficult childhood with his timid and alcoholic father, George. His mother, Augusta, was verbally abusive toward him and very controlling, but young Gein idolized the woman. His adoration for his mother was so intense that it bothered Gein's older brother, Henry, who occasionally questioned why the boy was so obsessed with the woman.

Gein's mother was obsessively religious and throughout his childhood he was subjected to her maniacal preachings about the sins of carnal desire and lust. In 1915, Augusta moved the family to a farm in

Plainfield, Wisconsin. Gein would only ever leave the farm to attend school.

In 1940, Gein's father died and the family lost the small income the man had brought into the household. Gein and his brother started to pick up odd jobs in order to support the family.

Gein lived with his parents well into his adult years. He never dated women, as his mother had him entirely convinced that doing so would be his path to hell.

In 1944, Gein's brother Henry died in a mysterious fire at the family farm. He had reported his brother as missing, but when police arrived he was able to take them straight to the man's body. An autopsy would reveal bruising on Gein's brother's head, but there was insufficient proof to take the matter any further, so his death was ultimately ruled an accident.

The following year, Gein's mother died and Gein was left alone on the family property. His obsession with his mother had never waned and he cordoned off certain areas of the home and turned it into a shrine to his mother (John Philip Jenkins, 2018). While these shrine-like areas remained completely untouched as an ode to his mother, the rest of the house fell into complete disrepair.

Gein's mother's death seemed to prompt the complete disintegration of the man's already fragile mental health.

The Murders Begin

After his mother's death, Gein supported himself with odd handyman jobs and also—terrifyingly—the occasional babysitting gig!

Gein came to the attention of local police in 1957 when a woman named Bernice Worden went missing. The hardware store owner had last been seen with Ed Gein who would regularly purchase items from her store for his handyman jobs. Worden went missing from her shop, along with her cash register, and a trail was left of blood leading out the store. The woman's son was a deputy sheriff and had always been highly suspicious of the strange Ed Gein.

Police visited the Gein Farm and found Bernice's body hanging from a ceiling. She had been shot and decapitated.

The discovery would also lead police to find that Gein had been hoarding a rather horrific collection. He had been robbing graves and collecting body parts which he used to make household items like lamp shades, clothing, and masks. He had practiced necrophilia with some of the body parts.

It would also emerge that Gein had killed another woman whose body was also found on the farm. Mary Hogan had run a tavern in the area which Gein frequented and she had disappeared in 1954 (John Philip Jenkins, 2018).

Police would attempt to link him to other murders and disappearances in the area, but no conclusive links could be made.

Investigation and Conviction

Gein admitted to killing both women and claimed that they had reminded him of his mother, who he both loved and detested in equal measures. He would plead not guilty by reason of insanity. Toward the end of 1957, Gein was found unfit for trial and over the next few years he would be confined to several different psychiatric institutions.

The following year, the Gein farm was razed to the ground in an unexplained fire.

In 1968, it was determined that Gein was fit to participate in his own defence and he was put on trial for the murder of the two women. Although he would be found guilty of having killed Bernice Worden, he would also be declared to have been insane at the time of the crime and was remanded to a psychiatric hospital. In 1974, Gein petitioned to be released, but when this failed he would not make news again until his death from cancer and respiratory illness in 1984 (John Philip Jenkins, 2018).

Although Gein was only conclusively linked to two murders, the body parts of at least nine other people were found on his property. Unfortunately, it could not be determined for certain whether these victims had been taken from graves or, in fact, murdered by Gein.

Despite the relatively low victim count which can be attributed to Gein, he would go down in history as one of the most reviled killers of his time. His crimes would inspire several movie characters including Buffalo Bill of *The Silence of the Lambs* and Leatherface in *The Texas Chainsaw Massacre*.

It is undoubtedly Gein's bizarre and terrifying use of human body parts that earns him our number one spot on this list. Although many of the killers we have discussed here have committed gruesome crimes, Gein's obsession with turning body parts and skin into household items makes him a terrifying character.

The Hall of Horror

With our top ten most notorious serial killers of all time complete, there are still quite a few terrifying criminals that deserve a mention. With any other topic, these could be called "honorary mentions," but considering our subject matter, we will call the list that follows, the "Hall of Horror."

Andrei Chikatilo

Chikatilo was a Russian serial killer who was given the monikers, "The Butcher of Rostov," and the "Rostov Ripper." His murder spree began in 1978 and by the time he was arrested in 1984, he would confess to raping and murdering 56 women and children. He would kidnap his victims and then kill them by slitting their throats. Chikatilo was executed for his crimes in 1994.

Albert Fish

In the 1930s, Albert Fish would become known as the "Boogeyman" because he was every child's worst nightmare. Although he would claim to have killed as many as 100 children, the courts could only convict him of three murders. Fish sent a horrifying letter to the parents of one of his victims describing in great detail how he had kidnapped, sexually assaulted, murdered, dismembered and cannibalized their 9-year-old daughter. Fish was executed by electric chair on January 16th, 1936.

Aileen Wuornos

Although a very low percentage of serial killers are female, one of the most infamous killers belongs to the "fairer" gender. Aileen Wuornos had a very difficult upbringing which included sexual abuse. She would go on to work in the sex trade as an adult where she started to lure men, rob, and murder them. She was convicted of seven murders in 1992 and executed by lethal injection in 2002.

Belle Gunness

Another female serial killer whose sadistic crimes earn a mention here is Belle Gunness who, in the 1880s, was known as "Lady Bluebeard." Although no one knows for certain how many men Belle actually killed, the confirmed number is 15. Her first two victims were her husbands, who were killed for insurance payouts. Thereafter, she would place ads in newspapers for potential suitors and when the men arrived at her farm, they were never seen again. Her crimes were only uncovered after her own apparent death in a fire on the farm. Legend has it, though, that the body found in the fire, along with those of her children, was not that of Belle Gunness and that the woman actually escaped and continued her life elsewhere.

Joachim Kroll

This German serial killer was believed to have murdered at least 14 people including his own children. Kroll was active between 1955 and 1976 and would strangle his victims, perform necrophilia on their bodies, and then cannibalize parts of them. His crimes were discovered when the pipes in his apartment building became blocked and the plumber discovered that the blockage was caused by human body parts.

Gilles de Rais

De Rais is one of the earliest recorded serial killers. He was a wealthy knight in the French Army and rode into battle alongside the likes of Joan of Arc. Between 1432 and 1433, De Rais killed at least 40 children. Cruelly, he would lure hungry children to his estate and then sexually assault and murder them. His acts were discovered when the bodies of several boys were found in his estate in 1437.

References

Biography.com Editors. (2017, April 28). *Harold Shipman.* Biography. https://www.biography.com/crime-figure/harold-shipman

Biography.com Editors. (2021, May 26). *H.H. Holmes Biography* [Review of H.H. Holmes Biography]. Biography.com. https://www.biography.com/crime-figure/hh-holmes

Biography.com Editors. (2017, April 28). *Jeffrey Dahmer.* Biography. https://www.biography.com/crime-figure/jeffrey-dahmer

Biography.com. (2017, April 28). *John Wayne Gacy.* Biography. https://www.biography.com/crime-figure/john-wayne-gacy

Biography.com editors. (2014, April 2). *Pedro Alonzo Lopez.* Biography. https://www.biography.com/crime-figure/pedro-alonso-lopez

Biography.com Editors. (2014, April 2). *Ted Bundy Biography.* Biography; A&E Television Networks. https://www.biography.com/crime-figure/ted-bundy

Biography.com Editors. (2014). *Charles Sobhraj.* The Biography Channel website. http://www.biography.com/people/charles-sobhraj-236026.

Biography.com Editors. (2017b, October 11). *Richard Ramirez.* Biography. https://www.biography.com/crime-figure/richard-ramirez

History.com Editors. (2018, August 21). *Jack the Ripper.* HISTORY; A&E Television Networks. https://www.history.com/topics/british-history/jack-the-ripper

Jenkins, J. P. (2019). *Harold Shipman* | Biography & Facts. In Encyclopædia Britannica. https://www.britannica.com/biography/Harold-Shipman

John Philip Jenkins. (2018). *Ed Gein* | Biography, Crimes, & Facts. In Encyclopædia Britannica. https://www.britannica.com/biography/Ed-Gein

The Editors of Encyclopedia Britannica. (2019). *Richard Ramirez* | Biography, Murders, Trial, & Facts. In Encyclopædia Britannica. https://www.britannica.com/biography/Richard-Ramirez

Printed in Great Britain
by Amazon

15534107R00047